SAP ECC AND S4 HANA

A Comprehensive Guide and
Preparatory Tips on Migrating
From SAP ECC to S4 HANA

JACOB A. PLUMMER

Table of Contents

INTRODUCTION

(Overview of SAP ECC AND SAP HANA)

OVERVIEW OF SAP ERP CENTRAL COMPONENT (ECC)

SAP ECC, or SAP ERP Central Component, was SAP's prior generation of enterprise resource planning software. SAP ECC combines numerous modules into a single, customizable solution that may run on any database the user chooses. An organization that uses SAP ECC can improve its business operations in the areas of finance, logistics, human resources, product planning, and customer support.

SAP ECC is a modular system. Businesses can use the components they need and arrange them as their landscape dictates. On a customized technological stack, SAP ECC can also work with third- party or customized applications. This versatility, however, is not without its drawbacks. Because each component of the landscape interacts with the others, a change in one will have an impact on how the others work. As a result, it's critical to thoroughly test your landscape before implementing any expansions, add-ons, customizations, or upgrades.

It's also worth noting that SAP ECC has reached the end of its life cycle. SAP plans to stop supporting SAP ECC in 2027. They are already planning to phase down ECC and encourage SAP ECC users to migrate to SAP S/4HANA.

SAP ECC implementations are a significant barrier for any customer due to the danger of changing how they manage critical information and processes; yet, the relevance of these systems, as well as the benefits of a successful/integrated ERP implementation, are far too valuable.

Modules can communicate with one another to provide a fully integrated solution tailored to practically any customer across a variety of industries.

SAP ECC is one of the favored solutions for many firms, with modules such as Financials (FI), Material Management (MM), Sales and Distribution (SD), and Human Capital Management (HCM), among others.

SAP ECC is most commonly used in medium and large businesses, and it was designed for a wide range of industries, including medicines, chemicals, and steel, as well as fast-moving consumer goods. SAP Business Suite is built on top of it, and it includes components, or modules, such SAP Customer Relationship Management and SAP Supply Chain Management.

When SAP went from R/3 to SAP ECC, it officially switched from using the term module to using the term component, but many in the industry still use the term module.

SAP ECC components have been linked together so that they can work together. Both module and component refer to a segment of the software that is designed independently to handle a certain set of business procedures (see figure). ECC is made up of two technological components and ten functional core components, or modules.

Below are frequently implemented functional modules that SAP ECC includes and the business functions they cover.

FICO

SAP FICO (SAP Finance and SAP Controlling) is actually made up of two modules that deal with financial accounting and reporting and cost planning and monitoring, respectively. They let organizations to manage and retain all of their financial data and transaction history in one place, as well as do financial analytics, by working together.

Sales and Distribution (SD)

The SD module is in charge of the primary sales and distribution processes. Selling items or services directly to clients or through distribution networks falls under this category. Customer returns, billing, and credit issuance are all handled by SD.

Materials Management (MM)

The MM module is in charge of managing supplier procurement of products and services, as well as related inventory procedures including counting and reconciling physical inventory. All goods issuance, receipts, and transfers of a material from one factory or storage place to another are likewise managed by MM.

Production Planning (PP)

The PP module assists organizations in aligning demand with manufacturing capacity, allowing them to better plan product manufacturing, sales, and distribution. PP is an important component of a manufacturer's supply chain since it can be used for discrete, process, repetitive, or a combination of these types of manufacturing.

Quality Management (QM)

The procurement, production, sales, and equipment maintenance operations are all heavily integrated with the QM module. Managing entire internal or external audits is one of the advanced features. QM may also assist in determining the fundamental reasons of product failure in order to ensure that a company's business processes continue to improve in quality.

Plant Maintenance (PM)

The PM module keeps an eye on machines and functional areas like a chiller room or boiler room to make sure they're in good operating order. When faults are found, it sends out alerts to avert machine failures and production disruptions. The SAP PM component covers business operations such as preventive, corrective, and refurbishment maintenance.

Customer Services (CS)

The CS module manages the business operations for providing customer equipment maintenance services. CS also has the ability to bill clients for the maintenance services provided.

Project System (PS)

PS is designed to handle large, complicated projects like establishing a new manufacturing plant or tracking a plant's maintenance turnaround time. By funneling all project-specific procurement or production through PS, this module can accurately allocate project costs while staying inside budget.

Human Capital Management (HCM)

HR-related functions are managed by the HCM module. Payroll, time management activities like attendance and leave, career development, travel, and workplace safety are all included. Submodules in functional modules can be implemented as needed.

SAP ECC Technical Components

For an ECC implementation, the technological components ABAP and NetWeaver were required. The ABAP component allows for custom development that is specific to a business. It was used by businesses to create custom reports or reporting formats to meet legal or financial reporting obligations.

The NetWeaver component is used to manage the system. It allows businesses to assign roles and permissions to individuals or groups.

SAP ECC Implementation

SAP is putting a lot of effort into S/4HANA. Companies who introduced SAP ECC, on the other hand, were faced with a significant task that necessitated the SAP-focused project implementation approach known as the ASAP (Accelerated SAP). Project planning, building a business design of reformed operations, ECC configuration and development, final preparation, and go-live and support were all major milestones.

Companies usually start with the functional modules FICO, Materials Management, and Sales and Distribution, though they can pick and choose which ones they desire. For example, a customer may have decided not to use SAP Project System after consulting with a SAP installation partner since it does not manage a big number of projects.

This amount of personalization and choice provided a lot of flexibility, but it also added a lot of complexity. SAP is attempting to persuade businesses to use cloud versions of S/4HANA, which standardizes products but limits flexibility. To make up for the lack of flexibility given by ECC, SAP is producing industry-specific versions of S/4HANA.

Future of ECC

SAP is pressuring businesses to adopt S/4HANA while committing to support ECC and other key Business Suite 7 apps until the end of 2027, with extended maintenance available until the end of 2030.

OVERVIEW OF S4 HANA

SAP's current enterprise application suite is SAP S/4HANA. The platform, which was first deployed in 2015, is widely regarded as the most significant update to SAP's core capabilities since the R/3 system was introduced in 1992. Under the name SAP Simple Finance, SAP S/4HANA was first introduced as a next-generation financial solution at the 2014 SAPPHIRE NOW technology conference in Orlando, Florida. SAP stated nine months later that it was expanding the core of the solution to become a full-scale enterprise resource planning platform, dubbed the suite SAP S/4HANA, and added certain main lines of business to the end of the name (e.g., SAP S/4HANA Finance).

SAP S/4HANA received logistics capability in four major areas in 2016: sourcing and procurement, manufacturing, supply chain, and asset management. Extended warehouse management (EWM) and production planning/detailed scheduling (PP-DS) capability were embedded directly into SAP S/4HANA, which was a significant improvement over SAP ERP.

Warehouse Management from SAP ERP to SAP S/4HANA EWM

In 2017, SAP added machine learning capabilities to the suite, making it easier to reconcile goods and invoice receipts and automate invoice assignments. Transportation management capability was integrated into SAP S/4HANA in September of that year. Predictive accounting was added to the system in 2018, and successive updates brought clever technological upgrades in the areas of artificial intelligence, blockchain, and the Internet of Things.

SAP has released multiple industry-specific SAP S/4HANA offerings: energy and natural resources, service industries, consumer industries, discrete industries, financial services, and public services. An embedded human resources line of business is in development as of 2021, and SAP has released multiple industry- specific SAP S/4HANA offerings: energy and natural resources, service industries, consumer industries, discrete industries, financial services, and public services.

SAP S/4HANA Innovations

SAP S/4HANA is an ERP business suite based on the SAP HANA in-memory database that enables businesses to conduct real-time transactions and analyze data.

A brownfield installation entails modernizing an existing SAP environment while keeping some legacy components in place. Because it requires a software update, some data translation, and some business process adjusting, it's similar to a regular upgrade. It's still disruptive, but not nearly as much as a brand-new deployment.

This method may be preferable if you are risk hesitant, prefer to use S/4HANA's capabilities gradually, or are concerned about the expenses of a greenfield implementation.

Companies who want to preserve their existing business operations more or less the same as previously should use the brownfield method. Some components of the migration process are more automated than in a greenfield deployment; for example, master data will be transferred to the new system without the need for heavy lifting.

SAP's approach for enabling customers to undertake digital transformation, a broadly defined process in which they can modify existing business processes and models or build new ones, is centered on S/4HANA. This enables businesses to be more adaptable, responsive, and resilient in the face of shifting business needs, customer demands, and environmental conditions. This S/4HANA-based business environment is referred to as the intelligent enterprise by SAP.

S/4HANA features

S/4HANA was created with a simpler data model, lean architecture, and a new user experience based on the tile-based SAP Fiori UX to make ERP more modern, faster, and easier to use. S/4HANA includes or integrates a number of sophisticated technologies, including artificial intelligence (AI), machine learning, Internet of Things (IoT), and advanced analytics. S/4HANA can help solve complex problems in real time and analyze more data faster than prior SAP ERP systems because to the SAP HANA in-memory database architecture and the integration of modern technologies.

S/4HANA on-premises can also be installed in public or private clouds, or as a hybrid. SAP S/4HANA Cloud is a multi-tenant SaaS version that differs from the on-premises version in terms of modules and functionalities. Over its older sibling, SAP S/4HANA introduced a slew of new features. The construction of a new code base, as well as the use of SAP HANA's in-memory computing architecture, which allows for real-time business statistics and analytics, and the convergence of transactional and analytical systems, were all significant advances.

New Functionality

Financials users could now access a single source of financial truth where both financial and management accounting documents were housed, thanks to new features like the Universal Journal. Better reporting, simpler access to KPIs for managers, and cockpits customized to specific end users to assist them make more informed decisions resulted as a result of this. SAP Fiori applications were created to give employees a better user experience by providing them with more visibility into operations and business data than conventional T-codes could.

Improved business processes such as predictive accounting were introduced to the system as soon as capability was fleshed out, thanks to the advent of intelligent technologies such as machine learning and process automation.

Simplification List

While SAP S/4HANA introduced plenty of new features, it also worked to improve parts of the existing SAP ERP suite as well as prior SAP S/4HANA releases. These improvements are detailed in the "simplification list" for each SAP S/4HANA version, which is a lengthy (sometimes 1,000+ page) document that outlines what was improved and why it is a better alternative for consumers than earlier capability.

SAP S/4HANA Lines of Business

SAP S/4HANA has reorganized core modules found in SAP ERP into what it calls lines of business (LoBs). Current or planned LoBs are discussed below.

SAP S/4HANA Finance

The SAP S/4HANA Finance LoB focuses on a company's financial activity. Financial accounting, control, treasury and risk management, financial planning, financial closing, and consolidation are all part of this process.

SAP S/4HANA's SRM and SCM Offerings

Supplier relationship management and supply chain management solutions previously present in the SAP Business Suite are included in this collection of modules that make up the SAP S/4HANA logistics LoBs. SAP did this on purpose to better distribute functionality and group processes that are related. Here's where you can learn more about SAP S/4HANA's logistics capabilities.

SAP S/4HANA Sourcing and Procurement

The SAP S/4HANA Sourcing and Procurement LoB is concerned with the activities surrounding the acquisition of raw materials required to complete orders. Extended procurement, operational purchasing, and supplier and contract management are all part of this.

SAP S/4HANA Manufacturing

The SAP S/4HANA Manufacturing LoB is concerned with the process of product creation. Manufacturing responsiveness, production operations, scheduling and delivery planning, and quality control are all part of this.

SAP S/4HANA Supply Chain

From pre-planning manufacturing runs to shipping items to customers, the SAP S/4HANA Supply Chain LoB focuses on overall business planning tasks. Production planning, batch traceability, warehousing, inventory management, and transportation management are all included.

SAP S/4HANA Asset Management

The SAP S/4HANA Asset Management LoB is concerned with the upkeep of a company's fixed assets, which range from tools and machinery to structures. This includes things like plant upkeep and EHS monitoring.

SAP S/4HANA Sales

The SAP S/4HANA Sales LoB is responsible for all actions related to the fulfillment of sales orders. Pricing, sales inquiries and quotes, sales contracts and agreements, free-of-charge orders, available-to- promise checks, incompletion checks, repair orders, individual requirements, return authorizations, credit and debit memo requests, picking and packing, billing, and revenue recognition are all included in this category.

SAP S/4HANA R&D/Engineering

The SAP S/4HANA R&D LoB focuses on the product lifecycle. This comprises defining the product structure and bill of materials, product lifecycle costing, portfolio and project management, innovation management, chemical data management, and other sensitive materials management, as well as being compliance with safety and health standards.

SAP S/4HANA Human Resources

SAP is actively developing the SAP S/4HANA Human Resources LoB, with an on-premise solution scheduled for 2022. Customers can use SAP S/4HANA with SAP Success Factors to create a cloud- based HR service in the meanwhile.

SAP S/4HANA Deployment Options

There are multiple avenues through which SAP S/4HANA can be deployed. Here's a brief overview of each.

On-premise

Traditional in-house IT infrastructure models are included in a SAP S/4HANA on-premise deployment. This deployment model covers a SAP S/4HANA instance that is physically hosted on the customer's premises. Customers can opt for a system conversion (brownfield) implementation, which converts an existing SAP environment to SAP S/4HANA; a new (greenfield) implementation, which migrates existing business data into a brand-new SAP S/4HANA system; or selective data transition, which employs shell conversion to reuse existing ERP processes in the new system.

Cloud

There are several cloud deployment alternatives for SAP S/4HANA, all of which require external cloud connection.

An SAP S/4HANA Cloud deployment places a customer's instance of the solution on a partitioned cloud server alongside other customers, providing SAP S/4HANA capabilities. Because of its uniform structure, the functional scope is constrained.

A private cloud deployment allows customers to use SAP S/4HANA without having to worry about the technical backend. It's ideal for enterprises that already have cloud experience and infrastructure, as it allows them to host the solution on their own cloud rather than

sharing space with other tenants, like the typical SAP S/4HANA Cloud deployment does.

The SAP S/4HANA Cloud or SAP S/4HANA deployed on a private cloud are both available with the RISE with SAP license.

Hybrid

In a hybrid SAP S/4HANA instance, on-premise and cloud deployments are combined. This could be done for a variety of reasons, such as to test the feasibility of both instances or to host an on-premise deployment at headquarters while using a cloud deployment at a satellite office.

SAP S/4HANA Release Cycle

SAP S/4HANA is updated several times a year. On-premise deployments are updated once a year, usually in September, while cloud-deployed instances are updated quarterly.

The four-digit year/month naming standard is used for SAP S/4HANA releases. The 2102 release of SAP S/4HANA Cloud, for example, refers to the release that was released in February 2021 (21). (02).

SAP has stated that it will continue to maintain ECC under a normal support contract until 2027, but if you wait until then to start moving to SAP S/4HANA®, you may meet a brick wall.

Moving to SAP S/4HANA gives your company access to next-generation operations on a proven technology platform that will support business growth, laying the groundwork for emerging technologies like embedded AI, an in-memory HANA database, real-time advanced analytics, and a FIORI interface, to name a few. By taking advantage of the benefits of transitioning to S/4HANA sooner rather than later, you can be a visionary, remain ahead of the competition, and transform legacy data into actionable insights.

Why Move to SAP S4 HANA

Moving to SAP S/4HANA allows your company to benefit from next-generation operations on a proven technology platform that will support business growth, laying the groundwork for you to take advantage of emerging technologies like embedded AI, an in- memory HANA database, real-time advanced analytics, and a FIORI interface, to name a few. By reaping the benefits of moving to S/4HANA sooner rather than later, you can be a visionary, stay ahead of your competition, and transform legacy data into actionable insights.

Upgrading to a new software solution can be difficult, but the benefits it can give to your company make it worthwhile. SAP S/4HANA enables businesses to benefit from advancements like as incorporated real-time analytics, SAP Fiori's latest user experience across all platforms, and faster reaction times and improved performance. Businesses can gain access to hundreds of new features and functionality by upgrading to SAP S/4HANA, including real-time supply chain, machine learning applications, finance, and predictive MRP, as well as state-of-the-art warehousing solutions.

Improve current business processes

With S/4 HANA Business-houses, you can "Reimagine Business" in terms of Reimagined Business Models, Reimagined Business Processes, and Reimagined Business Decisions.

The ability to connect with people, devices, and business networks in a "simple and fast" manner will help businesses work toward a simplified and flexible Business Model. With IoT, Big Data Analytics, Hybrid scenarios (cloud and on-premise applications), and native integration and connectivity with various business networks (such as Ariba, Hybris, and others), SAP S/4 HANA will make the world a playground for doing business.

The ability to "process simple" by very limited (and only if business requires) batch processing, job scheduling, and monitoring reduces latency or delay in receiving important information, allowing businesses to operate and processes work in real-time and on live data. The online, real-time availability of information, as well as the power of faster and smarter processing, will enable business-houses to think about "what is happening NOW" as well as how it can impact the immediate future, paving the way for "predictive analytics" and "what-if-simulations" scenarios and ways of doing business.

The "simple and real-time processing" will result in "reimagined business decisions," which will compare how decisions are made today to how they can be improved in the future. Businesses can expect to save time and money because there will be less "manual consolidation" of data. Most decisions made in "real-time," "on-the- fly," and with the assistance of "predictive analytics" and "what-if- simulations" will result in better control and decision making.

The integrated and simplified data-model will enable "decisions based on a single source of truth," as well as "drill-down to the highest level of granularity and easy viewing and linkage between KPI and its underlying transactional data."

The advantages of Simplified User Experience (Ux) via FIORI Applications for Business Users will be numerous. It will improve employee productivity and influence business results by allowing them to complete tasks at any time and from any location. It would also aid in the reduction of work completion time. Easier user interfaces will result in faster adoption of business processes. It would also reduce or eliminate the need for user training.

Based on HANA-LIVE Analytics, FIORI SMART Applications will assist Business Leaders in improving management productivity, streamlining processes, and influencing business results. Because of the reduced reliance on "desktop-only" environments and the increased ability to quickly approve via any device from anywhere on the network, it would help reduce travel, procurement, and other costs that normally add up due to process approval delays. It would also free up employees' time spent on administrative tasks, allowing them to focus on more creative and high-value tasks.

Retail and CPG, as well as many other industries, can benefit in the area of Sales & Marketing by focusing on increasing margins through real-time Price and Order Management. This is possible because the system can simulate prices and margins at any time, anywhere, and at any level of granularity. It would also support the development of real-time pricing quotes for customers and prospects, integrated with the ability to promise/deliver commitments.

Utilities companies can benefit from fuel supply chain optimization by lowering fuel costs and shortening order-to-delivery times. This could be made possible by an integrated supply chain, which connects suppliers and buyers through business networks and allows for faster and more accurate reconciliation of production capacity and demand. Plants and grids can improve their operational efficiency by increasing asset availability and reducing unplanned outages. SAP S/4 HANA would assist in providing a single, real- time view of plant and business performance, and business-houses would be able to analyze asset performance in real-time. The Utility Grid will be transformed into a "Intelligent Grid" by reducing energy waste and eliminating energy shortages, optimizing energy consumption through smart meters and demand-side management, and optimizing operational performance through the convergence of IT/OT systems and big data processing.

Gain a competitive advantage

Get a leg up on the competition by installing SAP S/4HANA, which has a slew of new features and applications that make the system's core even smarter. Before you risk falling behind, close the gap between your current and your future. Customers who upgrade to SAP S/4HANA will get access to a significantly reduced IT architecture, allowing them to modify their business models more easily. Real-time analytics help you make better decisions, and the new SAP Fiori applications provide you a better user experience.

Because you are not the only entity in the industry pursuing digital transformation, it is very likely that your SAP ECC competitors have already begun the upgrade process. As a result, getting ahead of your limited capabilities, finding an ERP testing service provider, and aiming for something new may help you perform better.

Furthermore, the time frame for use on SAP ECC will allow you to learn the situation, work on improvements, and ensure that you are on the right track with SAP HANA implementation. It will not only help you leverage productivity until SAP ECC support ends, but it will also help you uncover advanced capabilities on your business plan.

Simplify Your Landscape

Every business is unique, with different starting and ending points. Our experience ranges from implementing a brand-new solution to digitizing an existing landscape in the cloud, on-premise, or a hybrid of the two. We have worked with enterprises of all sizes, industries, and technology processes for any deployment type. We will assist you in keeping your business running while transitioning to new solutions.

SAP Landscape Transformation for S/4HANA is ideal for large enterprises with multiple SAP and non-SAP ERP systems, as well as customers who want to consolidate into a single global SAP S/4HANA system or migrate selective data.

Customers who want to consolidate their landscape or carve out selected entities or processes into an existing SAP S/4HANA system or Customer-specific migration project reusing standard migration content can choose SAP LT as a migration path to SAP S/4HANA.

The revolutionary in-memory column-store based capabilities of SAP HANA form the foundation of S/4HANA innovation, allowing both OLAP (analytical) and OLTP (transactional) data to reside in one system, allowing for real-time, LIVE analysis, reporting, simulation, and prediction, leading to smarter and faster business decisions. The key to success in those analyses is to carefully review all of your processes and adhere to best practices as much as possible, from Procurement-to-Pay all the way to Order-to-Cash and so on, at the risk of looking at data on your screen that does not reflect the true numbers.

Less development, more standardization, and best practices will allow you to consume those products more efficiently, and those products may be the answer to previous developments. Take advantage of this opportunity to ask "why not?" and encourage your company to simplify. It will free up your IT department to work on items that add real value to the business and to be more innovative, rather than coming to the office and spending the entire day coding, repairing code, or thinking about what needs to be changed in the program to accommodate an acquisition, a merger, a new tool that the company is considering purchasing, and so on.

Many people regard SAP S/4HANA as a once-in-a-lifetime career opportunity... I know many people who are proud of their R/2 –> R/3 project, but the fact is that there is a huge difference between moving from ECC to S/4HANA and moving from R/2 to R/3. S/4HANA allows you to not only improve what you already have, but completely re-imagine what is possible for your company in the coming years.

Many enterprises have massive data landscapes that have grown unwieldy over time, either as a result of acquiring companies and never fully merging systems, or as a result of divesting business units and leaving that data in the system rather than purging it. The reason for the data accumulation in both cases is that cleaning it up is too expensive, but as a result, these organizations are saddled with enormous baggage in the form of unused, siloed, and outdated data.

This is where the true value of S/4HANA is most apparent. The digital transformation itself – merging systems, cleaning data, migrating historical data, and aggregating all trusted data into a single structure – is what harmonizes these massive, highly customized data sets. That's where S/4HANA's embedded analytics come in, providing real-time actionable insights from your data to help you better optimize business processes and track and control costs.

S/4HANA is a business transformation, not just a technical upgrade. The outcome is intended to alter the way your teams operate and their day-to-day tasks. As a result, the motivation for embarking on a S/4HANA migration cannot be technical, such as SAP service deadlines or platform features. It has to be because you want a more comprehensive digital transformation of your business, and S/4HANA will play a key role in that.

To reap the full benefits of S/4HANA, you must integrate your ERP systems and consolidate your data into a single SAP database. That's what digital transformation entails. Without it, your S/4HANA migration will become bogged down in the same swamp of negative ROI that so many other ERP projects do.

Invest In Your Growth Strategy

If your company is growing, whether it's via entering new markets or expanding production facilities, you'll need software that can adapt and grow with you. Knowing that your existing ERP solution has a shelf life and that keeping up with the latest trends and advances will be more expensive, investing in an intelligent ERP system like SAP S/4HANA can support and complement your growth strategy while reducing time-to-market.

Future-proof your IT investment

As the 2027 deadline approaches, the more time you invest in your legacy ERP, building more integrations, customizations, and developments, the more difficult it will be to migrate to SAP S/4HANA. The SAP S/4HANA system is designed to work with SAP HANA, an in-memory database that allows for a drastically simplified data model and lightning-fast performance. It also offers an excellent user experience with SAP Fiori, which ensures a consistent appearance and feel across the whole ERP system, boosting employee happiness and productivity. S/4HANA will get all future SAP R&D expenditure, making it the optimal solution for your IT investment because you'll always be exposed to the latest technology and solution offerings.

Strategies For SAP ECC To S4-HANA Conversion

When enterprises wish to adopt SAP S/4HANA, they have two options: a greenfield strategy (new implementation) or a brownfield approach (old implementation) (System Conversion; Re-use).

As a result, the greenfield and brownfield approaches represent two distinct ways to convert a SAP ERP system to S/4HANA: Companies that choose the greenfield strategy install the SAP S/4HANA system from the ground up. Brownfield refers to a software upgrade that keeps all data and settings intact.

There's also selective migration, which is a kind of middle ground between greenfield and brownfield development (formerly: landscape transformation). The color field technique or a hybrid strategy are also mentioned by experts.

Selective migration is a brownfield-based strategic approach. If a company chooses this path, SAP professionals will duplicate the old system and convert it to S/4HANA without the data. Data migration is used to populate this empty system with legacy data. Individually, the migration can be managed: The experts may, for example, relocate only a certain part of data or recode data.

When it comes to implementing S/4HANA, the problem for businesses is determining the best implementation approach in the first place.

THE GREENFIELD APPROACH
What does Greenfield mean?

The Greenfield method denotes a fresh start, a fresh start with SAP S/4HANA "on a Greenfield site." This entails extensive reengineering as well as the prospect of comprehensive process simplification. This is based on the most recent technological breakthroughs. The Greenfield method ensures that the new implementation adheres to SAP standards and best practices.

During the implementation, all processes and systems are thoroughly reinstalled and configured. All environmental systems will be reviewed and, if necessary, replaced during this process.

Companies can put existing in-house innovations and third-party systems to the test with the new implementation, and see if these functions aren't already present in the SAP S/4HANA core and best practices.

Traditional in-house core system developments are no longer relevant. They are being phased out in favor of new architectures. These architectures, on the other hand, can only be created using the Greenfield method. Furthermore, the new designs enable a piece of software to be continuously modernized through frequent and rapid updates.

Whereas in the past, significant updates were used to renew vast portions of the program, today the focus is on ongoing updating of subareas. This implies that, because the program is totally refreshed every few years, no big new installations are required.

Because the present SAP system - for example, SAP ERP 6.0 - will continue to operate in parallel with the changeover until the new S/4HANA system is go-live, this strategic approach will have no impact on current business processes.

The Greenfield strategy is for anyone who wishes to fully utilize SAP S/4HANA's capabilities while also improving data quality.

SAP S/4HANA is the foundation for future business models and technology. Those who rely on Greenfield want greater freedom, more innovation, better data quality, and faster, leaner operations.

The greenfield method is a brand-new solution that allows you to create systems and workflows from the ground up. If your firm does not currently use a SAP ERP (such as ECC 6.0), the greenfield approach will apply immediately; nevertheless, organizations that are already using SAP can also choose this option. It gives the push to develop fresh new procedures in place of outmoded processes and inconsistent data. As a result, greenfield transitions are frequently accompanied with a change in organizational structure or business strategy.

Data does not have to be fully lost in a greenfield transfer, even if the system is wholly new. It's feasible to migrate data from the old system, and if switching on a specific date isn't convenient for your organization, both the old and new systems can run in parallel throughout the transition period.

Both new and existing clients can benefit from the Greenfield approach. Companies might explore the Greenfield method, especially if their present systems are highly varied and complicated. Only he can make the shift to S/4HANA's "new world" with SAP Best Practices. It also allows organizations to get rid of obsolete workarounds and provide them more flexibility in the future.

BROWNFIELD

A Brownfield strategy allows you to move to SAP S/4HANA without having to start from scratch and disrupting existing processes, by leveraging existing SAP landscape pieces such as supplier and partner interfaces. A brownfield implementation of S/4HANA necessitates a comprehensive migration of legacy environments. Consolidating and re-building a new SAP landscape is a cost-effective and risk-free option.

A Brownfield conversion offers a risk-free way to integrate the SAP landscape rebuild with the overall consolidation and harmonization of all SAP-related business operations at a low cost.

A system conversion, sometimes known as a "brownfield" approach, is an implementation strategy that involves converting an existing SAP ERP system to SAP S/4HANA. This means that once the conversion is complete, an organization's existing master and transactional data, custom development objects, and system customizations will be migrated to their new SAP S/4HANA system. This is in contrast to a new implementation (or greenfield implementation), which is an alternative approach companies take when they decide to build their SAP S/4HANA system from the ground up; or a hybrid implementation, which combines aspects of both greenfield and brownfield implementations and varies by company.

In most circumstances, a conversion may be accomplished in a single step; however, if your system is older than SAP ERP 6.0, you'll need to undertake a two-phase process. The first step in the two-phase scenario is to upgrade your system to a supported source release. After that, you can convert it to SAP S/4HANA.

It's crucial to note that not every system can be converted to SAP S/4HANA in its current state, as there are a number of requirements to meet. Add-ons and all business operations, for example, must be compatible with the new system. If they are incompatible, you must either remove the incompatibilities before converting or go with the greenfield method.

Because you're transporting existing data to a new site rather than having to recreate your landscape, a brownfield approach is often less expensive. You can avoid having to re-engineer procedures by incorporating legacy data into your SAP S/4HANA system. Your master data is automatically transferred to the new system, saving you the time and effort of having to extract and load it as if you were starting a new project (the greenfield option). Another benefit of a brownfield approach is that it allows you to clean up and remove obsolete custom code, as well as reduce your data footprint through data archiving.

5 steps to prepare your brownfield migration to SAP S/4HANA

During the preparation phase, your current SAP ECC system will be enabled to carry out the migration to S/4HANA.

Prepare a project plan for your own Brownfield migration.

However, before beginning the technical parts of a conversion project, we propose beginning with a planning phase to define the parameters (e.g. scope, schedule, budget, project structure) and ensure that the entire project team is on the same page in terms of technical aspects and procedure. Following that, the stages for completing a brownfield project might begin.

Take a look at the System Requirements.

- The first step is to review the system requirements:
- Is your system unicode-enabled?
- Is a Dual Stack Split required?
- Is a database update required?

Maintenance Planner (MP)

Following that, the MP, a SAP tool, will verify that the installed components, add-ons, and business operations are S/4HANA compatible. It also creates the download files that the Software Update Manager (SUM) will need at a later date to complete the migration.

The conversion to SAP S/4HANA will be approved if all checks were successful. If the MP cannot find a legitimate migration path (for example, because an add-on is not certified for S/4HANA), the migration will be stopped.

Item Check for Simplification

The simplification item check that follows identifies critical activities that must be accomplished in order to enable for the system's technical migration and to ensure that business operations continue to run after the SAP S/4HANA migration is complete. This includes various plausibility checks (such as in asset accounting) that detect SAP system irregularities. A full log contains information about errors as well as potential solutions.

Migration of the Custom Code

The study of advancements (Z programs, additions, and modifications) as well as information on where the code is incompatible with the new data structures are all part of the custom code migration. At this point, it's a good idea to make a priority list of which changes are either absolutely necessary or optional as soon as feasible.

Many of customers work with obsolete custom development projects. If this is the case, we propose using the ABAP Call Monitor (SCMON) to perform a thorough study of the system and eliminating any obsolete coding or programs that are no longer in use.

There are also some cross-module tasks, such as adjusting authorizations for FIORI use, as well as module-specific tasks. For example, before converting the logistics processes in SAP, the customer master data and supplier master data must be turned into Business Partners.

Selective Data Transition

To migrate to SAP S/4HANA®, the SAP S/4HANA® Selective Data Transition is an alternative to a System Conversion and New Implementation. This strategy combines the benefits of both approaches without their drawbacks: take advantage of S/4HANAadvancements ® while carefully utilizing and repurposing your existing investment. Selective Data Transition allows you the freedom to change your SAP S/4HANA® system's customizations, data, and processes.

Data Management and Landscape Transformation (DMLT) services are used in a selective data transfer to migrate "selected" data from the current SAP ERP system to the new SAP S/4HANA environment.

The phrase "selected" is frequently used to indicate a data migration that is limited in scope, such as master data, open items, and balances. In terms of technique, breadth, and business interruption, this is not what the SAP S/4HANA® Selective Data Transition approach is about.

Benefits of a selective data transition

- Customers can combine several SAP ERP systems into a single SAP S/4HANA system,
- Allowing them to reuse and redesign applications.
- A phased implementation reduces the hazards associated with a big-bang strategy.

The Experts

SAP has developed an expert group of partners - the SAP S/4HANA® Selective Data Transition Engagement – to provide SAP clients with a trustworthy and proven migration approach in their migration to SAP S/4HANA®. This working group, which was formed in 2018, brings together system landscape transformation experts from CBS, Datavard, Natuvion, SAP, and SNP.

The goal of this working group is to define and adhere to shared standards, methodologies, and processes for a secure and flexible migration to SAP S/4HANA® in collaboration with SAP. Through effective standardization, the five firms hope to provide excellent quality, decreased risk, shorter time to value, and lower costs of SAP S/4HANA® migrations.

You can select the following data for the transition: Shell Conversion

The team uses this method to generate a clone of the existing PROD environment that is devoid of master and transactional data but contains the ABAP Repository and settings (Customizing). The team uses this method to generate a shell copy of the existing PROD environment, which includes the ABAP Repository and configuration (Customizing) but no master or transactional data. The project team converts this shell copy to a SAP S/4HANA instance via system conversion. The conversion process is easier and faster in the absence of master and transactional data. In addition, the team may quickly change the simplification list items without affecting the business data.

Client Transfer

To transfer to the target SAP S/4HANA system, you select a client and the underlying master and transactional data with the configuration (Customizing).

Company Code Transfer

You can use this method to create a single client on the new SAP S/4HANA system by selecting a company code from the present setup. To move to the new environment, you can select the client's master or transactional data. Alternatively, you can migrate to the target environment by selecting the configuration (Customizing) with or without the master data.

System Merge

You can join business data from two or more clients to create an empty SAP S/4HANA instance using the system merge procedure. These clients can come from the same SAP ERP system or from different SAP ERP systems.

SAP Activate Methodology

SAP Activate Methodology is a modular and agile framework that assists project teams with the particular actions that must be delivered in each phase of the project by offering accelerators that make the task of a deliverable easier to complete and workstreams that span multiple phases. The SAP Activate Methodology is a next- generation agile strategy that combines a reference solution built for continuous innovation with ready-to-run business processes tailored for S/4HANA software implementations. It allows for an iterative process with frequent validations. It also includes S4HANA migration, integration, and setup best practices. It can handle a variety of deployments, including fresh deployments, system conversions, and landscape transformations. In its implementation technique, activate comprises six separate phases.

Different phases

The Activate implementation methodology consists of the following phases:

- Discover phase
- Prepare phase
- Explore phase
- Realize phase
- Deploy phase
- Run phase

Discover phase

The first part of the Activate approach assists you in developing a plan and implementation methods. SAP offers a free trial with pre-configured best practices scenarios for both cloud and on-premise implementations. During this phase, business users analyze various business processes across the enterprise functions using S/4HANA on-premise (30 days trial) and cloud (14 days trial) solutions. It also allows users to create a business case for implementing SAP S/4 HANA

Prepare phase

The project team does the first planning and preparation efforts to get the project started in the Prepare phase. The team develops project goals, scope, and a project strategy during this phase. The project team's duties and tasks are also outlined. Aside from these, this phase includes tasks such as establishing project standards, organization, and governance, customer team assessment, project management, delivery monitoring and reporting systems, team orientation, and system access.

Explore phase

The project team ensures that business requirements can be addressed within the solution and project scope during the Explore phase. To make this step easier, a preconfigured SAP best practice solution with client solution scope is employed, and solution validation workshops are held. Data requirements evaluation, data cleansing, establishing configuration settings, and determining master data and organizational setup needs begin the integration with legacy systems.

Realize phase

Based on the inputs from the preceding processes, the project team employs a series of iterations in the Realize phase to construct and test a comprehensive business and system environment. The end-to-end testing of the solution is conducted by the business user, who also sets a cutover plan. They also take the stakeholders through the solution process. This phase also includes activities such as solution configuration, change management planning, and end-user training. During this phase, the project team also performed Data Volume Management (DVM), data migration and verification, security implementation, IT infrastructure setup, and sizing and scalability verification.

Deploy phase

In the Activate technique, the Deploy step is critical. The project team prepares and executes the system for production release during this phase (Go-Live). The team is in charge of the cutover plan, transitioning business processes to the new system, and transitioning from implementation to production support. The team performs the final dress rehearsal and production cutover that was prepared earlier in the phase to guarantee a smooth transition. Following the system's release, this phase concludes with hyper-care activities.

Run phase

The Run phase concludes the Activate methodology. During this stage, the project team completes all activities and transfers all details to the support team. The team was also involved in the system's last-minute bug or error fixes. This phase concludes the integration with the SAP

Solution Manager for operations, monitoring, and support. The project team completes the project and distributes all relevant documents to the business owners.

Why is SAP Activate necessary?

The implementation of SAP has long been considered costly and complex, for example, for implementations of SAP ERP. With SAP Activate, SAP now offers a standardized implementation solution for SAP S/4HANA. This reduces the complexity of implementation projects.

Unlike previous projects, SAP Activate, for example, eliminates the usually time-consuming blue print phase - saving time and money. In addition, customers are already intensively involved during the project and can get to know the new system in demo systems and help develop it. The benefits become apparent earlier, and the risks are reduced.

S4 HANA Cloud Vs On Premise

What is SAP S/4HANA Cloud

SAP S/4HANA Cloud is a full enterprise resource planning (ERP) system with intelligent technologies such as AI, machine learning, and advanced analytics built in. It enables businesses to adopt new business models, manage rapid business change, orchestrate internal and external resources, and leverage AI's predictive power. Benefit from tight, native process integration, industry depth, and a consistent in-memory data model.

SAP S/4HANA Cloud is the SAP S/4HANA ERP system delivered as a Software-as-a-Service (SaaS). It is a collection of integrated business applications that allow for the planning of company resources based on the needs of the company. This suite is also available as cloud ERP software with SAP S/4HANA Cloud.

The SAP S/4HANA Cloud, billed as the "intelligent ERP system of the next generation," was first introduced in February 2017. The provider of an ERP system as a cloud-based software version provides companies with a solution that does not rely on their own resources such as internal hardware, databases, and IT expertise.

Users can virtually connect their departments and functional areas, digitize their business processes, and thus adapt to new development trends more quickly.

SAP S/4HANA Cloud is powered by the SAP HANA in-memory database. This high-performance analysis application, which was previously only available in conjunction with various hardware before the SAP cloud solution, uses artificial intelligence to analyze large amounts of data, among other things.

The development and integration platform's in-memory technology enables users to access data more quickly and "in real time," thereby speeding up processes. This is also possible with the SAP Cloud Platform.

SAP S/4HANA Cloud has numerous advantages, particularly for small and medium-sized businesses. Many technical or financial requirements, for example, that would be required to implement a traditional on-premise solution are eliminated. But what exactly is the case for using SAP cloud ERP software?

Flexible subscription

The subscription model involves paying a monthly fee to use the SAP cloud platform. This is proportional to the number of users.

Users have the ability to add or remove users from the subscription as needed. Additional maintenance costs, on the other hand, are never incurred.

Fast implementation

SAP S/4HANA Cloud can be implemented more quickly. The user receives the pre-built platform in a standard version, so no custom programming is required. Furthermore, no prior knowledge is required to use the user interface.

Increase efficiency

SAP best practices enable users to implement standardized, tried-and-true resource management processes and procedures. Analysis and business processes are simplified and accelerated as a result. Individual roadmaps are also available for industry-specific functions.

Maintenance and support

Customers no longer have to worry about server capacity or software maintenance thanks to the SAP cloud platform. Because of integrated analysis tools and configuration, pricing, and offering functions, the development and support of new products and services is also possible with little effort..

Fast innovation cycle

Customers in rapidly growing businesses value adaptability and flexibility in particular. A quarterly innovation cycle is provided by SAP S/4HANA Cloud. As new innovations such as machine learning and predictive analytics become available, users can benefit from them.

The main pillars of SAP S/4HANA Cloud

The intelligent ERP system is built on three cutting-edge technologies. SAP created these, which enabled SAP S/4HANA Cloud to achieve company-wide process improvement and a smooth digital transition. The three foundations at a glance:

SAP Digital Assistant

SAP S/4Hana Cloud includes a virtual assistant, SAP CoPilot. The assistant can adapt to the user and their role based on contextualized information by using artificial intelligence. The use of ERP applications and functions is made easier by the natural interaction via voice and text commands.

SAP Machine Learning

Users can automate tasks with SAP S/4HANA Cloud's integrated machine learning. This is especially useful when tasks are repeated and errors could occur as a result of manual execution. Furthermore, automation means more time saved.

SAP predictive analytics

Informed decisions can be made quickly thanks to SAP Predictive Analytics in SAP S/4HANA Cloud. In fact, the analysis tool can forecast the outcomes of specific actions by analyzing all available data. The tool, in the form of individual applications, can be tailored to the needs and application areas of the user.

SAP S/4HANA On-Premise

SAP S/4HANA On-Premise is a version of the SAP ERP Business Suite that is built on the SAP HANA in-memory database platform. This is an internal platform that is hosted on your own servers and managed by your organization. As a result, you as a business manage and control everything, including the HANA database, applications, servers, networks, and other related systems. SAP S/4HANA On-Premise Edition is licensed in accordance with SAP's standard licensing model. It is an internal platform installed on servers or virtual machines managed by yourself or a trusted partner, and the application software is maintained by your company. SAP upgrades are released on an annual basis, and your team is responsible for implementing and testing the new releases.

SAP S/4HANA On-Premise can also be hosted in the Syntax Private Enterprise Cloud by a managed services provider such as Syntax. Syntax manages it for customers and offers a PaaS (platform as a service) solution.

The On-Premise Edition includes the full ERP functionality of SAP Business Suite, as well as simplifications for SAP Simple Finance and integrations with SAP Hybris Marketing, SAP JAM, and SAP Ariba Network.

The On-Premise Edition is ideal for businesses that require a comprehensive set of customizable features. This edition is appropriate for organizations that have established business processes and are looking for effective monitoring and configuration.

SAP S/4HANA On-Premise provides dedicated hardware and infrastructure hosted by SAP, a hyperscaler, or a data center. It has a Bring Your Own License and infrastructure subscription, which gives it more freedom and flexibility in service offerings. The customer is in charge of managing upgrades and determining the rate of adoption. Upgrades should be carried out on an annual basis.

SAP S4 HANA (HEC) has a full S/4HANA industry and country scope, with ERP-like customization, modification, and extensibility. SAP's on-premise deployment option, like S/4HANA Cloud (private), can be implemented using the new implementation method, system conversions, or selective data transition.

What Is The Difference Between SAP S/4HANA On-Premise And Cloud?

Companies interested in a S/4HANA ERP solution can select between S/4HANA Cloud and S/4HANA On-Premise. Both models are built around the SAP Fiori design concept, which aims to simplify and personalize the user experience. While their functionality is very similar, the variants differ in their implementation and handling.

We've already covered all of the S/4HANA deployment options, but let's take a look at the key differences between the SAP cloud and on-premise versions.

Deployment options

SAP S/4HANA Cloud - Public Cloud

The SAP S/4HANA Cloud's most common variant is classified as Software-as-a-Service (SaaS). This means that the ERP system is hosted on the provider's server and is fully managed by the provider. In general, it entails:

- Subscription-based software use rights
- SAP manages software
- Multitenant Software-as-a-Service environment

SAP S/4HANA Cloud - Private Cloud

In addition to the public cloud, there is a private version available in the form of the SAP S/4HANA Enterprise Cloud (HEC). Because the customer receives their own server from the service provider, this is also known as Infrastructure-as-a-Service (IaaS). Despite the fact that this is a private SAP cloud, the system is still managed by the provider. In general, it entails:

- Perpetual or subscription-based software rights
- SAP provides hardware, operations services, and optional application
- Single-tenant environment

S/4HANA On-Premise

Customers who use the ERP solution S/4HANA On-Premise host the application on their own server. Users must first purchase it in the form of a traditional licensing model before they can implement it on their internal hardware.

With S/4HANA On-Premise, the customer manages all areas, including the HANA database, data centers, and networks, as well as the software's maintenance and development. This may imply greater adaptability, but it may also imply greater effort. Which updates or support packages are required is also at the discretion of the customer. In general, it entails:

- Perpetual software use rights
- Customer responsible for hardware, implementation, and ongoing operations

Licensing models

In addition to the flexible deployments mentioned above, SAP provides different licensing models: perpetual licenses, subscription licenses, and consumption-based term licenses.

SAP S/4HANA Cloud - Public Cloud

All SAP software deployed in the cloud is available via a subscription-based license model, with an annual subscription fee paid as part of a term contract. Subscription terms are typically three to five years long. In general, it entails:

- Term license - typically 3 to 5 years
- Annual subscription (recurring) fee based on estimated use — includes everything: software use, database, maintenance and support, hardware, and application management
- Available for cloud solutions primarily (SAP S/4HANA; SAP C/4HANA; SAP Concur®, SAP Ariba®, and SAP Success Factors® solutions; SAP Cloud Platform, and SAP BusinessObjects solutions)

SAP S/4HANA Cloud - Private Cloud

SAP S/4HANA's private cloud uses a consumption-based model for all SAP software deployed in SAP's public cloud. In general, it entails:

- Term license

- No annual commitment; payment based on actual usage — includes everything: software use, database, maintenance and support, hardware, and application management

- Available for selected cloud offerings (SAP Cloud Platform, SAP Ariba®, and SAP Fieldglass® solutions)

SAP S/4HANA On-Premise

The on-premise perpetual license grants customers perpetual use of software rights to an agreed-upon quantity of software. You have the option of using "Classic" SAP software or SAP S/4HANA- branded software. In general, it entails:

- Perpetual software use rights

- One-time license fee — includes software use rights and database

- Annual recurring support fee — includes maintenance and support

- Available for on-premise scenarios primarily (SAP ERP®, SAP S/4HANA®, SAP C/4HANA, and SAP BusinessObjects® solutions)

For instance, if a company has 3,000 employees and authorizes 150 of them to use SAP, the company will only have to pay a license fee once and only for those 150 employees.

This method includes tools for selectively transferring configuration and custom code from older ERP systems to SAP S/4HANA by migrating the database, applying software updates, and converting data from third-party data models to the new, SAP-specific S/4HANA data model. Customers can use the SAP Solution Manager to manage the design of their projects.

PREPARING FOR MIGRATION

Re-evaluating your business needs is one way to prepare for an S4/HANA migration. Because your company relies on the SAP ERP system on a daily basis, consider the specific business processes that run on SAP. This will assist you in determining what you need from a migration as well as what technical debt is currently present in your system that should be reduced or eliminated.

Another aspect of reevaluating business need is determining which functionality will be migrated as-is, what will be enhanced or modified as part of the migration and digitization process, and what will be completely excluded from the migration. These features are either obsolete or being completely replaced by a newer version.

Users and business experts should be included in the migration process so that testing can be improved through feedback sessions and regular communication about the migration itself. This improves transparency throughout the process, resulting in a more successful and efficient migration solution.

Make Performance and Security a Priority

Before, during, and after a migration, the performance and security of a system should always be prioritized. What is there if your system isn't efficient, agile, and secure?

Make sure to include software experts on your team to improve both performance and security during the migration process. A focus on security and performance requirements during migration and delivery will reduce the risk of downtime and security vulnerabilities.

Consider the Ecosystem

Another aspect to consider in preparation for an S4/HANA migration is the larger ecosystem in which your SAP system is embedded. SAP systems frequently integrate with other systems, and if an integration fails, your company's ability to complete business tasks may be jeopardized. To avoid this, ensure that your testing throughout migration includes the entire landscape of systems in your ecosystem— the SAP systems, the systems on which they rely, and the systems on which they rely.

The transition to SAP S/4HANA is fraught with challenges and unknowns that can be overcome with proper planning. It is worthwhile to make the effort because switching to the new system provides significant opportunities for your company to increase the digital value added of its processes and activities. The time has come to take the initiative and prepare for digital transformation.

If you are planning to migrate to S/4HANA, there are some preparatory steps you can take right now. Implementing these steps gives you significant advantages later in the transition project and allows you to enjoy many S/4HANA world functions in your current SAP landscape.

In the following step, you choose the best implementation scenario for you (Greenfield or Brownfield) and decide how the systems will be operated, i.e. in the cloud, on premise, or in a hybrid scenario. You create your own SAP S/4HANA Roadmap based on your decision. Then, working with an experienced IT consultant, you migrate to the new ERP system more quickly and securely.

Preparatory Tips

There are some helpful tips on how to prepare for the SAP S/4HANA migration and which concrete measures are already profitable for your company and will significantly accelerate and facilitate migration. For this purpose, useful evaluation tools such as the SAP Readiness Check for S/4HANA, the SAP Transformation Navigator, and the Process Discovery for SAP S/4HANA Transformation are available (former Business Scenario Recommendation Report).

These tools can be used to independently analyze your processes ahead of time and provide recommendations for any necessary action. For more information on these tools, please contact the FIS experts, who will be happy to assist you. You will find information on five practice-oriented preparatory measures for the switch to S/4HANA in the sections below.

1. PREPARE CUSTOM CODING FOR YOUR TRANSFORMATION

Custom Code Lifecycle Management (CCLM) is a process that analyzes your individual code for quality, frequency of use, and optimization options. For this purpose, you can use the S/4HANA readiness check, a tool available in the SAP Support Portal that can be used to determine where and to what extent conflicts arise as a result of S/4HANA simplifications. This, in turn, affects the changeover variant (Brownfield vs. Greenfield) and the required time. As a result of the check, you will receive actionable recommendations in cases where a custom code migration is required.

The Usage Procedure Login, or its successor, the Source Code Monitor, can be used to analyze at a deep level which modification are not required or used in day-to-day operations and slim the system accordingly. "Housekeeping" and removing unnecessary ballast are thus critical for a smooth transition. These procedures aid in identifying and making necessary adjustments prior to the start of the project, which speeds up the project's progress.

Your benefit when migrating to SAP S/4HANA:

- Proactively avoiding error sources and delays in the transition project
- Reduced effort for the S/4HANA transition
- Improved performance – already present in your current SAP system landscape

2. CHECK THE PERFORMANCE OF YOUR IT ARCHITECTURE

Check your readiness in advance using the Readiness Examine your IT architecture to see if it is ready for S/4HANA. To ensure that the necessary prerequisites for the new Business Suite have been met, the current system landscape must be compared to the requirements of the S/4HANA environment. This prevents time lags later in the transition project. The following components should be included in a preliminary check: IT infrastructure (including system sizing, networking, and security), backup strategy, and monitoring.

Your benefits of a migration to SAP S/4HANA:

- Ensured smooth operation during migration
- Simplified SAP landscape
- Modernization of your operating tools

3. UPDATE YOUR FORMS IN SAP

SAP Smart Forms and SAP Script from SAP ERP ECC 6.0 will not be developed further in the medium term by SAP. The most significant advantages of Adobe Interactive Forms are interactivity and the use of the PDF format. Data can be directly entered and transmitted to the ERP system in a visually appealing and user-friendly format. Using Adobe's SAP Interactive Forms, you can also easily and intuitively design the layout of quotations, orders, and invoices, for example. As a result, numerous new (mobile) solution scenarios are possible.

To avoid delays later in the transition project, SAP ERP forms should be ported to the latest version as soon as possible. Your company already benefits from interactive forms and will be able to use the revised layout after the migration. When compared to previous technologies, Interactive Forms simplifies, flexible, and intuitive layout design. This expands your options for professionally implementing your corporate design in the system.

Your benefit when migrating to SAP S/4HANA:

- Reduced adjustment effort when transitioning to S/4HANA
- Enhanced layout options for fonts and design
- Increased flexibility due to the connection of your systems to the Adobe Document Server

- Improved interactivity due to the use of forms: data transfer directly to the back end system or to a worklist for checking in advance

- Mobile usage scenarios: a mobile use of the forms in the cloud is also possible without any problems

4. ADJUST YOUR USER INTERFACES FOR SAP S/4HANA IN ADVANCE

Many user interfaces in your current software environment can already be adjusted to new technologies to ensure higher labor productivity and efficiency. The SAP Business Client, in conjunction with SAP Fiori apps, is one of the user interfaces that will need to be tweaked in this case. The SAP Readiness Check also assists you in determining which Fiori apps are recommended for you. These apps can be tailored to specific user requirements and SAP landscapes, allowing for flexible and simple use by all users. Topics such as Usability Engineering have efficiency potential and can be used to increase overall user satisfaction in this context.

5. PROACTIVELY PROMOTE DIGITIZATION IN YOUR COMPANY

Take the initiative and begin dealing with the opportunities and challenges of digital transformation right away: How digitally advanced is your company? What work steps are digitizable? Create a structured Change Management process, integrate all corporate divisions involved in a timely manner, and proactively address challenges in your company at an early stage. The S/4HANA transition is not a one-off project affecting only one business unit. This is why the entire corporate infrastructure, as well as all processes and departments, must be considered and included.

The preparatory measures for the S/4HANA migration already provide benefits such as process improvements and performance boosts. The upcoming changeover is an excellent opportunity to examine internal business processes and, if necessary, optimize them. This enables you to continuously develop your company and capitalize on future innovative developments today.

POST CONVERSION TO S/4HANA

This is intended to provide readers with quick and concrete common post conversion to S/4HANA tips that they can include (if applicable) in their first conversion cycle and embrace as part of their conversion journey so that this potential issue does not arise during the production conversion.

- Technical Post conversion tips and suggestions
- Finance Post SUM Conversion tips and suggestions

Technical Post Conversion Tips And Suggestions

Conversion to SAP S/4HANA SUM Tool

SUM Logs: Examine the SUM logs for errors following the technical conversion.

Action:

- Check LONGPOST.LOG For A List Of Issues Encountered During The Conversion.
- BEFORE RESTARTING THE OPERATION, APPLY THE CORRECTIONS OR NOTES REPORTED FOR EACH ERROR.

Conversion to SAP S/4HANA Fiori

Applications availability: Ensure that Fiori Launchpad and applications can run properly after the conversion and upgrade.

Action:

- Run report /UI5/APP_INDEX_CALCULATE to update SAPUI5 application index

- Run report /UI2/GET_APP_DESCR_REMOTE_ALL to replicate app descriptors

- Invalidate cache such as transactions /UI2/INVALIDATE_GLOBAL_CACHES and /UI2/INVALIDATE_CLIENT_CACHES

Conversion to SAP S/4HANA Basis Tasks

Other key tasks: Following the conversion, several additional Basis tasks are required.

Action:

- Release suspended batch jobs, program BRCTRNS2

- Confirm new WF user is SAP_WFRT not WF-BATCH

- Review Workflow Configuration

- Activate business functions for Fiori: FIN_FSCM_CLM, FIN_FSCM_BNK, FIN_REP_SIMPL_2,FIN_REP_SIMPL3, FIN_REP_SIMPL4, FIN_LOC_SRF

- Execute SGEN

- Check HANA Log Mode – Change if necessary; undo parameter changes from FI data migration.

- Monitor ST22 and fix any ABAP dumps

- Review certificates pertaining to SSO, PSE regeneration if needed

- SSL certificates to use SAN (Subject Alternative Name) for Google Chrome Note 2725592
- Update NW kernel patch if required
- Implement SAP Note 2606478 REGENERATE_SAP_NEW, then, run the report

Conversion to SAP S/4HANA Data Handling

Obsolete Data Handling: After the conversion, how to delete obsolete data?

Action: Deletion rules delivered by SAP will run in PRD without business downtime, if you:

- Successful validated the system conversion
- Tested the deletion rules successfully in an appropriate test system (copy of PRD)
- Created a backup of database
- Deletion depends on data model change: rows or columns or entire tables

Recommended SAP Notes:

- SAP Note 2661837
- SAP Note 2190137

Finance Post SUM Conversion tips and suggestions Conversion to SAP S/4HANA Finance Migration

Dumps in MUJ execution: When the MUJ step is in execution, your SAP HANA Database starts maxing out on CPU usage and then generates dumps for out of memory situations.

Action:

Change DB parameters:

> ini -> [execution] –

>   >   max_concurrency_hint –

> set it to 20indexserver.ini [optimize_compression]
> row_order_optimizer_threads -> set it to 20

- Set Statement memory limit to 750 GB
- Change the code in stored procedure to include a hint ZCL_FINS_MIG_UJ_HDB_GENERATED=>CREATE_C ORRECTION

Recommended Notes

- SAP Note 2712348
- SAP Note 2811658

Conversion to SAP S/4HANA Finance

Deprecated transactions: After the conversion, transactions such as KA0, CPV1, KB21 etc. are deprecated.

Action:

- Use transaction ST03N to list transaction codes and programs used in the system in the past and check which ones have been replaced with newer transactions, programs, or WebDynpro applications.
- Adjust authorization roles for the relevant roles
- Consider the use of new Fiori Apps
- Find deprecated transactions in the simplification list.

Recommended Notes

- SAP Note 2270335
- SAP Note 2742613

Old Variants: After the conversion old variants are missing – not migrated automatically

Action:

- Execute report RSVCHECK to find out which variants are obsolete(Note 153865).
- Execute program RSVARDOC_46X or RSVARDOC_610 to adjust the obsolete variants.

Recommended Notes

- SAP Note 1953229
- SAP Note 241876

Note: DO NOT execute RSVARDOC_46X/RSVARDOC_610 towards all variants, please ONLY adjust the variants found by RSVCHECK. Otherwise unexpected issues may happen(like value lost.eg)

Conversion to SAP S/4HANA FSCM

House Banks: After the system conversion, transaction FI12 is not supported SAP S/4HANA 1610 and 1709. However, you want to re-enable this transaction code for a simple maintenance view of house banks.

Action:

- Implement note 2646577 to enable FI12 or upgrade to OP1809.

Note: that with this transaction, it is only possible to create House Banks like earlier.

- To create the House Bank Accounts you still have to access either the NWBC app or the Fiori App 'Manage Bank Accounts'. This transaction has links/buttons to launch the NWBC app for Create/Change based on the action you execute.

Recommended Notes

- SAP Note 2646577 Workaround A (preferred):

Assign SAP Standard Role "SAP_SFIN_CASH_MANAGER" to users.

Run transaction NWBC and open the "Cash Manager" cockpit Run "Manage Bank Accounts" app.

Workaround B:

Obtain WDA technical application name and configuration name from Fiori Apps library

Manually build access URL as follows: Use application

Check these SAP Notes:

- SAP Note 2424544
- SAP Note 2463516
- SAP Note 2752986

Conversion to SAP S/4HANA Finance UX

FIORI Embedded Analytics Report: FIORI Finance Embedded Analytics reports will not show data

Action:

Fiori Apps consume the new ABAP development model for S/4HANA meaning that some applications will be able to expose analytics information on their own. Hence to obtain a correct behavior you will need to setup the Embedded Analytics Engine.

Recommended Notes
- SAP Note 2289865
- SAP Note 1972819

www.ingramcontent.com/pod-product-compliance
Lightning Source LLC
LaVergne TN
LVHW051613050326
832903LV00033B/4480